JACKPOT JOKES

CANOPY BOOKS

© 2019 by Canopy Books, LLC
28 N Wisconsin Ave
N Massapequa, NY 11758

All rights reserved. No part of this publication may be reproduced in whole or in part, or stored in a retrieval system, or transmitted in any form, or by any means, electronic, photocopying, recording, or otherwise, without written permission of Canopy Books.

Made and printed in
Jiaxing, China
May 2019
Ages 5 & Up
ISBN: 978-1-946426-29-1

GET READY TO GIGGLE!

YOU HIT THE JACKPOT WITH THIS JOKEBOOK! MONEY CAN BE FUNNY, AND THE JOKES IN THIS SECTION PROVE IT! THESE PAGES ARE PACKED WITH PUNS, ONE-LINERS, KNOCK-KNOCK JOKES, RIDDLES, AND MUCH MORE THAT ARE GUARANTEED TO TICKLE YOUR FUNNY BONE. YOU CAN BET YOUR BOTTOM DOLLAR ON IT!

PUNNY STUFF

PUNS ARE JOKES THAT USE SOUNDALIKE WORDS OR WORDS WITH MORE THAN ONE MEANING. LET'S GET STARTED WITH SOME REALLY "PUNNY" STUFF!

Q: How do dinosaurs pay their bills?

A: *With Tyrannosaurus checks!*

Q: What is it called when you lend money to a bison?

A: *A buff-a-loan!*

Q: How do cows add up their money?

A: *With a cowculator!*

Q: What do you call a cow who goes bankrupt?

A: *An udder failure!*

Q: How many skunks does it take to cash a check?

A: A phew!

Q: Why did the sheep have to pay a traffic fine?

A: She made an illegal ewe turn!

Q: Why do cows need money?

A: To go to the mooooovies!

Q: When should you buy a bird?

A: When it's cheep!

Q: Why don't ponies make good auctioneers?

A: Because they're always a little horse!

Q: Why wouldn't the shrimp share his money?
A: Because he was a little shellfish!

Q: Why did the dog have to pay a fine?
A: He got a barking ticket!

Q: When a cow wishes for money, who does she ask?
A: Her dairy godmother!

Q: What does a buffalo get after dinner?
A: The buffalo bill!

Q: What do you call a kitten who counterfeits money?
A: A copycat!

Q: How many ants does it take to rent a house?
A: Ten ants!

Q: Why can't a leopard hide his money from the other leopards?
A: Because he's always spotted!

Q: What do fish use for money?
A: Sand dollars!

Q: What did the duck say to the cashier?
A: Put it on my bill!

Q: How do you stop an elephant from charging?
A: Take away his credit card!

Q: How did the clam pay for his new car?
A: He shelled out a lot of money!

Q: What type of horse will lend you money?
A: Broncos, because they always have a buck!

Q: How much money does a skunk have?
A: One scent!

Q: How do trees access their bank accounts?
A: They log in!

Q: What did the tree do when its bank closed?
A: It started a new branch!

CALL THE VET

GIRL:
"My dog swallowed a dollar."

FRIEND:
"Oh my gosh! Is he okay?"

GIRL:
"Seems like it. No change yet!"

NAILED IT OR FAILED IT?

WHEN IT COMES TO MONEY MANAGEMENT, DID THESE PEOPLE NAIL IT...OR FAIL IT? EITHER WAY, IT'S FUNNY!

Q: Why did the lady put her money in the freezer?

A: She wanted cold hard cash!

Q: Why did the man keep a clock in his wallet?

A: He wanted to spend some time!

Q: Why did the student eat his dollar bill?

A: His mother told him it was for lunch!

Q: Why did the girl put glue on her hands?

A: So money wouldn't slip through her fingers!

Q: Why did the boy throw money out of the window?

A: He wanted to see prices fall!

Q: Why did the man climb onto the restaurant's roof?

A: They told him his meal was on the house!

KNOCK, KNOCK!

KNOCK, KNOCK!
Who's there?
ANITA.
Anita who?
ANITA LITTLE MONEY!

KNOCK, KNOCK!
Who's there?
CANOE.
Canoe who?
CANOE LEND ME FIVE BUCKS?

KNOCK, KNOCK!
Who's there?
ORANGE.
Orange who?
ORANGE YOU GOING TO GIVE ME THAT FIVE BUCKS?

KNOCK, KNOCK!
Who's there?
HARRY.
Harry who?
HARRY UP! I REALLY NEED THAT FIVE BUCKS!

FOR RICHER OR POORER

SOME WOULD SAY THESE JOKES ARE RICH. OTHERS MIGHT SAY THEY'RE A POOR EXCUSE FOR HUMOR. WHAT DO *YOU* THINK?

Q: Why are bloodhounds rich?
A: *Because they're always picking up scents!*

Q: What do you get if you cross a sorceress with a millionaire?
A: *A very witch person!*

Q: Why are scarecrows rich?
A: *Because they're outstanding in their field!*

Q: Why are rivers rich?
A: *Because they have two banks!*

Q: Why are oceans rich?
A: Because they have lots of clams!

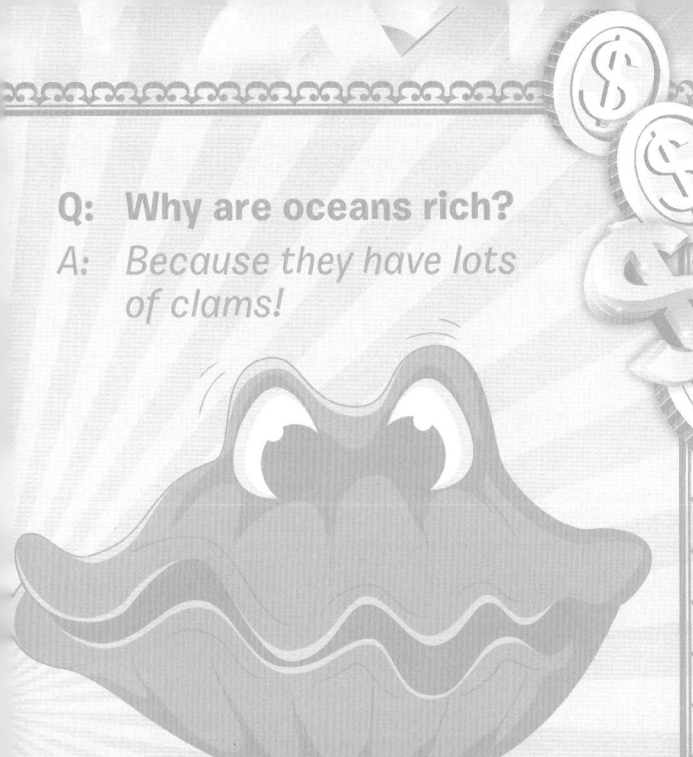

Q: Why are birds rich?
A: Because they have nest eggs!

Q: Why are lifeguards rich?
A: Because they're such good savers!

Q: What did the broke cat say?
A: "I'm 'paw'!"

Q: What did the gopher say when he lost all his money?
A: "Gopher broke!"

Q: What did the broke desk lamp say?
A: "Can you spare some change? I'm a little light."

Q: Why are toucans rich?
A: Because they have such big bills!

Q: Why are roosters poor?
A: Because they work for chicken feed!

Q: Why is a herd of female deer poor?
A: Because they don't have a buck!

Q: How did the broke farmer mend his pants?
A: With cabbage patches!

Q: Why was the coffee broke?
A: It was always getting mugged!

ONE OR TWO?

Little Angie was crying one day.

"What's wrong?" her mother asked.

"I lost my quarter," Angie sobbed.

"Oh, honey, don't be sad. Here's another quarter," her mother said.

Angie started crying harder.

"What's wrong now?" her mother asked.

"I wish I had told you I lost two quarters!" Angie wailed.

FREE RIDE

BOY:
"Hey, cabbie! How much for a ride to the airport?"

CABBIE:
"That'll be ten bucks."

BOY:
"I have a really big suitcase. How much for the suitcase?"

CABBIE:
"That's no charge."

BOY:
"Okay, just take the suitcase. I'll walk!"

YOU DON'T SAY

CAN YOU SPOT THE POPULAR SAYINGS OR PHRASES IN THESE JOKES?

Q: Why was the wallet so noisy?

A: *Because money talks!*

Q: Why can't you bend a quarter in half?

A: *Because change is hard!*

Q: What did the vending machine say when the quarter got stuck in it?

A: "Money's tight these days!"

Q: Why shouldn't you carry two half-dollars in your pocket?

A: Because two halves make a "hole," and you could lose your money!

Q: Why don't cows have any money?

A: Because farmers milk them dry.

Q: What did the palm tree do when it gave away its money?

A: It bid it a "frond" farewell!

Q: How did rich people get their money?

A: They were calm, and collected.

LONELY BILL

A wallet contained a $1 bill, three $5 bills, two $10 bills, and two $20 bills.

The $1 bill was miserable.

It felt singled out.

BORROWING MONEY

TED:
"Can you lend me $10?"

JOE:
"Sorry, I only have $5."

TED:
"That's okay. You can owe me the other $5!"

NEVER MIND

STOP US IF YOU'VE HEARD THIS ONE BEFORE...

Q: Did you hear the joke about the guy who shoveled a hole to bury his money?

A: *Never mind, you wouldn't dig it!*

Q: Did you hear the joke about the giraffe who found $20 in a tree?

A: *Never mind, it's way over your head!*

Q: Did you hear the joke about the guy who ate a $1,000 bill?

A: *Never mind, you wouldn't swallow it!*

Q: Did you hear the joke about the super-expensive college?

A: *Never mind, you won't get into it!*

Q: Did you hear the joke about the $1 bill that posted a Facebook update?

A: *Never mind, you wouldn't "like" it!*

Q: Did you hear the joke about the treasure that went down with the <u>Titanic</u>?

A: *Never mind, it's too deep!*

CROSSING THE ROAD

IF CHICKENS CAN DO IT...

Q: Why did the penny cross the road?

A: To get to the other side.

Q: Why didn't the nickel follow the penny?

A: Because it had more "cents"!

ILLEGAL CROSSING

A man was arrested for illegally crossing a road. He stood before the judge in court.

"I'll give you a choice. Thirty days or $100," the judge said.

"I'll take the $100. Thanks a bunch, Judge!"

LET'S COMPARE

DIFFERENT OR SIMILAR, ALL OF THESE COMPARISONS ARE FUNNY!

Q: What's the difference between a sailor and a shopper?

A: *One sails the seas and the other sees the sales!*

Q: What's the difference between a goose and George Washington?

A: *One has a bill on its face, the other has his face on a bill!*

Q: What do a baker and a millionaire have in common?

A: *They are both rolling in dough!*

Q: How is the moon like a dollar?

A: *They both have four quarters!*

BOOK 'EM

THESE JOKES ARE LITERALLY BY THE BOOK!

Q: Which book is worth the most money?

A: A checkbook!

Q: Where can you always find money?

A: In the dictionary!

Q: Why couldn't the letter B make any money?

A: It was always in a book and never in the office!

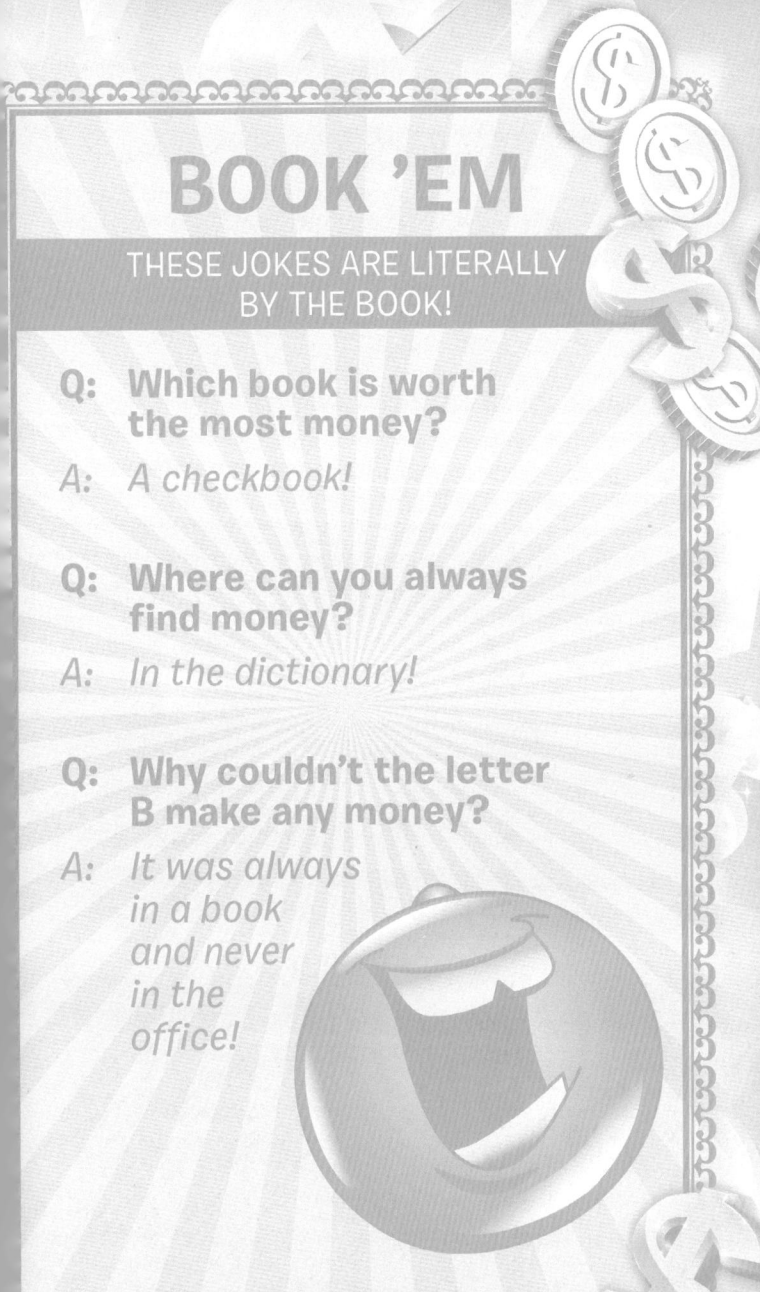

ON THE JOB

THESE JOKES ARE WORKING HARD FOR A LAUGH!

Q: Why did the elephant quit the circus?

A: He was tired of working for peanuts!

Q: Who makes a million dollars a day?

A: Someone who works in a mint!

Q: Why did the man throw his paycheck into the trash?

A: He wanted some disposable income!

Q: How did Sir Lancelot make money?

A: He worked the knight shift!

Q: Why did the man quit his job at the bank?

A: *He lost interest!*

Q: Did you hear about the cannibal lawyer?

A: *He charges an arm and a leg!*

Q: Did you hear about the origami store that couldn't make any money?

A: *It folded!*

Q: Did you hear about the big paddle sale at the boat store?

A: *It was quite an oar deal!*

Q: Why did the man lose his job at the orange juice factory?

A: *He couldn't concentrate!*

CASH IN ON THE LAUGHS

Money jokes aren't the only way to cash in! This next section is packed with more puns, riddles, and knock-knock jokes that are guaranteed to please...From food jokes to monster jokes, there's something for everyone. You've hit the jackpot of jokes! Just keep reading to unleash the laughs.

STRICT DIET

A man feels itchy all over, so he goes to the hospital. After examining him, the doctor gives him the bad news.

"You're completely infested. I've never seen anything like it. You have lice, ticks, fleas, and mites," he tells the patient.

"Oh my gosh!" the man replies. "What are you going to do?"

"Well, first, I'm putting you on a strict diet of pizza only," the doctor replies.

"How will that help?" the man asks.

"It won't...but it's the only food we can fit under the door!"

PIZZA AND PASTA

Everyone loves pizza and pasta, and you'll love these jokes too!

Q: Do you want to hear a pizza joke?
A: Never mind, it's too cheesy!

Q: What kind of pizza do dogs like best?
A: Pup-aroni!

Q: Did you hear about the sleeping pizza?
A: It was a piZZZZZa!

Q: What do you call a fake noodle?
A: An impasta!

Q: What did the angry pepperoni say to the cook?
A: "You want a pizza me?"

Q: What do you call it when pasta gets sick?
A: Mac and sneeze!

Q: How do you fix a broken pizza?
A: With tomato paste!

CROSSING THE ROAD

Why did the chicken cross the road? These jokes shed some light on this burning question.

Q: Why did the chicken cross the road?
A: To get to the other side!

Q: Why did the turkey cross the road?
A: To prove he wasn't chicken!

Q: Why did the rooster cross the road?
A: To cockadoodle doo something!

Q: Why did the gum cross the road?
A: It was stuck to the chicken's foot!

Q: Why did half a chicken cross the road?

A: To get to its other side!

Q: Why did the sneaky chicken cross the road twice?

A: He was a double crosser!

Q: Why did the turkey cross the road?

A: It was the chicken's day off!

Q: Why did the rubber chicken cross the road?

A: She wanted to stretch her legs!

Q: Why did the chicken cross the road?
A: BURP! What chicken?

Q: Why did the chicken cross the basketball court?
A: The referee was calling fowls!

Q: Why did the chicken cross the playground?
A: To get to the other slide!

Q: Why did the chicken cross the beach?
A: To get to the other tide!

Q: Why didn't the chicken skeleton cross the road?
A: It didn't have the guts!

Q: Why did the chicken cross the construction site?
A: She wanted to see a person lay a brick!

Q: Why did the chicken cross the clothing store?
A: To get to the other size!

Q: Why did the chicken cross the amusement park?
A: To get to the other ride!

Q: What was the farmer doing on the other side of the road?
A: Catching all the chickens!

CHEW ON THIS

The funny food jokes in this section will give you plenty to chew on. Your friends will eat them up!

Q: Why should you never tell jokes to eggs?
A: It cracks them up!

Q: How do you make a milk shake?
A: Give it a good scare!

Q: Why is it hard to keep secrets on a farm?
A: The potatoes have eyes, and the corn has ears!

Q: What's the best thing to put into a pie?
A: Your teeth!

Q: What is a pretzel's favorite dance?
A: The Twist!

Q: If a crocodile makes shoes, what does a banana make?
A: Slippers!

Q: Why did the tomato blush?
A: It saw the salad dressing!

Q: Why did the lettuce win the race?
A: It was ahead!

Q: Why did the boy put candy under his pillow?
A: He wanted to have sweet dreams!

Q: What day do potatoes hate the most?
A: Fry-day!

Q: What do you call a piece of bread that makes straight As?
A: An honor roll!

Q: What did one plate say to the other plate?
A: "Dinner's on me!"

Q: Why did the man eat snails?
A: He didn't like fast food!

Q: How do you help a sick lemon?
A: You give it lemon aid!

KNOCK, KNOCK!

KNOCK, KNOCK!
  Who's there?
Figs.
  Figs who?
Figs the doorbell – it's broken!

KNOCK, KNOCK!
  Who's there?
Lettuce.
  Lettuce who?
Lettuce in – we're cold!

KNOCK, KNOCK!
  Who's there?
Olive.
  Olive who?
Olive you!

PUNNY STUFF

Q: Why did the banana go to the doctor?
A: It wasn't peeling well!

Q: Why won't you starve in a desert?
A: Because of all the "sand which is" there!

Q: What do you call cheese that isn't yours?
A: Nacho cheese!

Q: Why was the man sorry he became a vegetarian?
A: He thought it was a big missed steak!

Q: Why do melons have fancy weddings?
A: Because they cantaloupe!

DOCTOR, DOCTOR!

A man goes to the doctor. He has a banana sticking out of one ear, a carrot sticking out of the other ear, and a green bean sticking out of one nostril.

"Doctor, I'm not feeling well," the man complains.

"Well, it's no wonder," the doctor replies. "You're not eating right!"

TOO COOL FOR SCHOOL

Brrrring, brrrrring! School's in session, and the subject today is comedy. Get your laugh on with these silly school-related jokes.

Q: Why did the student steal a chair from the classroom?
A: The teacher told him to take a seat!

Q: Why did the student study in the airplane?
A: He wanted a higher education!

Q: What's the best way to get straight As?
A: Use a ruler!

Q: Why did the teacher wear sunglasses?
A: Because his students were so bright!

Q: What's the difference between a teacher and a train?
A: The teacher says, "Spit out that gum!" and the train says, "Chew, chew!"

Q: Why did the student eat his homework?
A: Because he didn't have a dog!

Q: Why are math teachers unhappy?
A: They have lots of problems!

Q: What gets whiter and whiter as it gets dirty?
A: A chalkboard!

Q: What do you get when you cross a teacher with a vampire?
A: Lots of blood tests!

Q: What school subject do witches like best?
A: Spelling!

Q: What is the smartest state?
A: Alabama, because it has four As and one B!

Q: Why did the teacher write on the window?
A: To make the lesson very clear!

Q: Why did the student bring scissors to school?
A: He wanted to cut class!

Q: Have you heard about the cross-eyed teacher?
A: She couldn't control her pupils!

KNOCK, KNOCK!

KNOCK, KNOCK!
 Who's there?
BROKEN PENCIL.
 Broken pencil who?
**NEVER MIND—
 IT'S POINTLESS!**

KNOCK, KNOCK!
 Who's there?
DEWEY.
 Dewey who?
**DEWEY HAVE TO GO
 TO SCHOOL TODAY?**

KNOCK, KNOCK!
 Who's there?
ABE.
 Abe who?
ABE B-C-D-E-F-G!

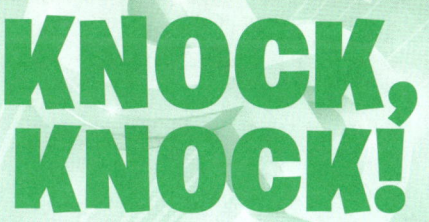

PUNNY STUFF

Q: Why was the broom late for school?
A: It overswept!

Q: Why did the clock get sent to the principal's office?
A: It tocked too much!

Q: How do bees get to school?
A: On the school buzz!

Q: Why did the geometry teacher miss school?
A: She sprained her angle!

Q: What is a math teacher's favorite dessert?
A: Pi!

100 PERCENT

"How did you do in school today?" asked Will's mom one afternoon.

"I got 100," Will answered.

"That's wonderful! What in?"

"A 60 in reading and a 40 in spelling!"

AMUSING ANIMALS

If it moos, barks, snorts, or trumpets, it's probably hilarious in some way! Check out these funny jokes about the always-amusing animal kingdom.

Q: Why do seagulls fly over the sea?
A: If they flew over the bay, they'd be called bagels!

Q: What do you call a bear with no teeth?
A: A gummy bear!

Q: How do you make a goldfish old?
A: Take away the "g"!

Q: What is as big as an elephant but weighs nothing?
A: An elephant's shadow!

Q: What's the worst thing about being an octopus?

A: Getting washed up before dinner!

Q: What did the leopard say after lunch?

A: "That hit the spot!"

Q: What do you call a cow with no legs?

A: Ground beef!

Q: What is black, white, and red all over?

A: A sunburned penguin!

Q: Why did the cow cross the road?
A: To get to the udder side!

Q: What do you get from a pampered cow?
A: Spoiled milk!

Q: What did the mama cow say to the baby cow?
A: "It's pasture bedtime!"

Q: What do you call cattle with a sense of humor?
A: Laughing stock!

Q: What kind of horses go out after dark?
A: Nightmares!

Q: Why did the pony go to the doctor?
A: He was a little hoarse!

Q: What do you call a horse who lives next door?
A: Your neigh-bor!

Q: What happened when the pig pen broke?
A: The pigs had to use a pencil!

Q: What do you call a pig lying down?
A: A groundhog!

Q: Did you hear about the pig who lost his voice?
A: He was disgruntled!

Q: How is a dog like a telephone?
A: It has collar ID!

Q: How do you stop a bull from charging?
A: Take away his credit card!

Q: Where does a 600-pound gorilla sit?
A: Anywhere he wants!

Q: How do you catch a squirrel?
A: Climb a tree and act like a nut!

Q: Did you hear about the lion who ate the clown?
A: He felt funny!

Q: What goes ticktock, bowwow, ticktock, bowwow?
A: A watch dog!

Q: Why did the elephant quit the circus?
A: It was tired of working for peanuts!

KNOCK, KNOCK!

KNOCK, KNOCK!
  Who's there?
COWS GO.
  Cows go who?
COWS GO MOO, NOT WHO!

KNOCK, KNOCK!
  Who's there?
CHICKEN.
  Chicken who?
JUST CHICKEN UP ON YOU!

KNOCK, KNOCK!
  Who's there?
QUACK.
  Quack who?
IF YOU QUACK ONE MORE BAD JOKE, I'M LEAVING!

PUNNY STUFF

Q: Why are chickens so bad at baseball?
A: They always hit fowl balls!

Q: Why did the cow cross the road?
A: To get to the udder side!

Q: Why did the bison go to the bank?
A: To get a buff-a-loan!

Q: What do you call a deer with no eyes?
A: No eye deer!

Q: What do you call an exploding monkey?
A: A baboom!

DO THE MATH

After a long day of work around the farm, a talking sheepdog gets the sheep back into their pen for the night.

"All forty sheep accounted for," he reports to the farmer.

"But I only have thirty-six sheep," the farmer replies, puzzled.

"I know," says the dog. "I rounded them up!"

SILLY SPORTS

You're guaranteed to score big with the sports-related jokes in this section. Every one is a winner!

Q: Why did the player bring string to the game?

A: So he could tie the score!

Q: Why did the golfer wear two pairs of pants?

A: In case he got a hole in one!

Q: Why did the man keep a surfboard near his computer?
A: He liked to surf the Internet!

Q: Why did the football coach go to the bank?
A: He wanted his quarter back!

Q: What gets harder and harder to catch the faster you run?
A: Your breath!

Q: What is the hardest thing about skydiving?
A: The ground!

Q: Why are babies like basketball players?
A: They're always dribbling!

Q: Why is Cinderella so bad at sports?
A: She always runs away from the ball!

Q: Why did the police go to the baseball game?
A: They heard someone was stealing a base!

Q: How do runners remember things?
A: They jog their memory!

Q: Why are soccer players so smart?
A: They know how to use their heads!

Q: How do athletes stay cool during a game?
A: They stand near the fans!

Q: Did you hear about the man who ran behind the car?
A: He got exhausted!

Q: Why is tennis so noisy?
A: The players raise a racket!

KNOCK, KNOCK!

KNOCK, KNOCK!
  Who's there?
ADOLF.
  Adolf who?
ADOLF BALL HIT ME IN DA MOUF, AND NOW I TALK FUNNY!

KNOCK, KNOCK!
  Who's there?
EUROPE.
  Europe who?
EUROPE TO BAT!

KNOCK, KNOCK!
  Who's there?
TENNIS.
  Tennis who?
TENNIS FIVE PLUS FIVE!

PUNNY STUFF

Q: Two waves had a race. Who won?
A: They tide!

Q: What is a cheerleader's favorite color?
A: Yeller!

Q: What is a horse's favorite sport?
A: Stable tennis!

Q: Why can't a bicycle stand up on its own?
A: Because it's "two tired"!

Q: Why is it a bad idea to play sports in the jungle?
A: There are too many cheetahs!

ONE POINT

Photos of basketball teams from past years hung in the high school hallway. Each photo was labeled with its year: 96-97, 97-98, and so on.

"It's such a shame," Ron said to his friend Jim one day as they passed the photos.

"What's that?" Jim replied.

"How our school always loses by exactly one point!"

OUT OF THIS WORLD

The space-related jokes in this section are truly out of this world. Prepare for a galaxy of giggles!

Q: What do you call a peanut in a spacesuit?
A: An astronut!

Q: What kind of plates do they use in space?
A: Flying saucers!

Q: Why didn't the sun go to college?
A: It already had a million degrees!

Q: Did you hear about the new restaurant on the moon?
A: Great food but no atmosphere!

Q: How do you know when the moon has had enough to eat?
A: It's full!

Q: What kind of music do planets sing?
A: Neptunes!

Q: What is a light-year?
A: The same as a regular year but with less calories!

Q: What do astronauts read for fun?
A: Comet books!

Q: Why did the star go to school?
A: It wanted to get brighter!

Q: Where does an astronaut park his spaceship?
A: At a parking meteor!

Q: Why is Saturn so rich?
A: It has lots of rings!

Q: Why are astronauts forgetful?
A: They're always spacing out!

Q: How do astronauts hold up their pants?
A: With asteroid belts!

Q: What was the first animal in space?
A: The cow that jumped over the moon!

KNOCK, KNOCK!

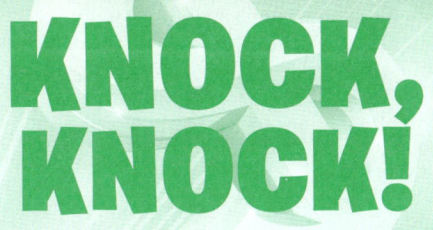

KNOCK, KNOCK!
   Who's there?
SHUTTLE.
   Shuttle who?
SHUTTLE THE DOORS— WE'RE READY TO LAUNCH!

KNOCK, KNOCK!
   Who's there?
ROCKET.
   Rocket who?
THE BABY'S CRYING— YOU BETTER ROCKET!

KNOCK, KNOCK!
   Who's there?
MISSION.
   Mission who?
I'VE BEEN MISSION YOU— COME OUT AND PLAY!

PUNNY STUFF

Q: How does the barber cut the moon's hair?
A: E-clipse it!

Q: How do you make a sandwich for an astronaut?
A: With launch meat!

Q: If runners get athlete's foot, what do astronauts get?
A: Missile toe!

Q: How do you throw a party for an astronaut?
A: You have to plan-et!

Q: What do metric aliens say?
A: "Take me to your liter!"

UNDER THE OPEN SKY

One day Mike and Rob go camping together. In the middle of the night, Mike nudges Rob and wakes him up.

"Look up. What do you see?" he says.

"I see hundreds of stars, and the moon, and the Milky Way," Rob replies.

"And what does that tell you?" Mike says.

"That the universe is huge and amazing?" answers Rob.

"No, silly. It means someone has stolen our tent!"

CREEPY, CRAWLY, AND COMICAL

Bugs, snakes, spiders, and other creepy-crawly critters are icky, scary...and hilarious! Turn your shivers into laughs with these silly jokes.

Q: Who always comes to a picnic but is never invited?
A: Ants!

Q: What do you call a fly without wings?
A: A walk!

Q: Why didn't the butterfly go to the dance?
A: Because it was a mothball!

Q: What do you call a lice-infested rabbit?
A: Bugs Bunny!

Q: What's worse than finding a worm in your apple?
A: Finding half a worm!

Q: Did you hear about the bed bugs who met in the mattress?
A: They got married in the spring!

Q: Why do spiders like computers so much?
A: They love the World Wide Web!

Q: What's the best place to buy bugs?
A: At the flea market!

Q: What do you do when two snails start a fight?
A: You just let them slug it out!

Q: Why are snakes hard to fool?
A: You can't pull their leg!

Q: What did the snake do when it got upset?
A: It threw a hissy fit!

Q: What has four wheels and flies?
A: A garbage truck!

Q: Why are spiders like tops?
A: They're always spinning!

Q: Why do bees hum?
A: Because they've forgotten the words!

KNOCK, KNOCK!

KNOCK, KNOCK!
  Who's there?
HONEYBEE.
  Honeybee who?
HONEYBEE NICE AND LET ME IN!

KNOCK, KNOCK!
  Who's there?
LARVA.
  Larva who?
I LARVA YOU!

KNOCK, KNOCK!
  Who's there?
ROACH.
  Roach who?
**I ROACH YOU A LETTER—
DID YOU GET IT?**

PUNNY STUFF

Q: Why did the fly fly?
A: Because the spider spied 'er!

Q: How do fleas travel?
A: They itch-hike!

Q: How do you make a glowworm happy?
A: Remove his tail–he'll be de-lighted!

Q: Which snakes are found on cars?
A: Windshield vipers!

Q: How do snakes put their babies to bed?
A: With a good-night hiss!

MAKE IT SNAPPY!

A man has a pet centipede. One day he asks the centipede to run an errand.

"Go to the store for milk, and make it snappy!" he says.

Over an hour later, much to the man's irritation, the centipede finally shows up with the milk.

"I thought I told you to make it snappy," the man says.

"Well, I had to put on my shoes first!"

ON THE JOB

Get ready to work the room with the sidesplitting jokes in this section. You're about to prove that comedians aren't the only ones with funny jobs!

Q: When do cops sleep on the job?
A: When they're undercover!

Q: What do lawyers wear to court?
A: Lawsuits!

Q: Who earns a living by driving their customers away?
A: Taxi drivers!

Q: Why was there thunder and lightning in the lab?
A: The scientists were brainstorming!

Q: Why did the man lose his job at the orange juice factory?
A: He couldn't concentrate!

Q: How did the barber win the race?
A: He took a short cut!

Q: How do chefs make their beds?
A: With cookie sheets!

Q: Why did the thief take a shower?
A: He wanted to make a clean getaway!

Q: Who would you hire to clean the ocean?
A: A mer-maid!

Q: What did the painter say to the wall?
A: "I got you covered!"

Q: What do postal workers do when they get mad?
A: They stamp their feet!

Q: What nails do carpenters hate to hit?
A: Fingernails!

Q: Why are cooks mean?
A: They beat the eggs and whip the cream!

Q: Why did the employee take the elevator to work?
A: He wanted a raise!

KNOCK, KNOCK!

KNOCK, KNOCK!
  Who's there?
NOAH.
  Noah who?
NOAH GOOD MECHANIC? MY CAR WON'T START!

KNOCK, KNOCK!
  Who's there?
COOK.
  Cook who?
HEY! WHO ARE YOU CALLING CUCKOO?

KNOCK, KNOCK!
  Who's there?
DWAYNE.
  Dwayne who?
CALL THE PLUMBER TO DWAYNE THE TUB!

PUNNY STUFF

Q: Why did the can crusher quit his job?
A: Because it was soda pressing!

Q: What did the janitor shout when he jumped out of the closet?
A: "SUPPLIES!"

Q: What is a dentist's favorite time of day?
A: Tooth hurty!

Q: When does a doctor get mad?
A: When he runs out of patients!

Q: Why did the baker stop making doughnuts?
A: He was bored with the hole business!

A DAY OFF

A teenager goes to see his boss at work one day.

"Tomorrow is spring-cleaning day," he says, "and my mom needs me to help her around the house—washing windows, sweeping floors, all that stuff."

"Sorry, kid. We're shorthanded. I can't give you the day off," the boss replies.

"Thanks, boss. I knew I could count on you!"

NATURALLY HILARIOUS

Mother Nature sure does have a sense of humor, and the jokes in this section put it on display. Go ahead and let 'em rip—you're a natural!

Q: How do you know the ocean is friendly?
A: It always waves!

Q: What bow can't be tied?
A: A rainbow!

Q: What falls but never hits the ground?
A: The temperature!

Q: What did the tree wear to the pool party?
A: Swimming trunks!

Q: Why did the leaf go the doctor?
A: It was feeling green!

Q: What has a mouth but can't eat?
A: A river!

Q: What did the ground say to the earthquake?
A: "You crack me up!"

Q: How do flowers greet each other?
A: "Hi, bud!"

Q: Why is grass so dangerous?
A: It's full of blades!

Q: What kind of tree fits in your hand?
A: A palm tree!

Q: How do you identify a dogwood tree?
A: By its bark!

Q: What did the tired shrub say to its friend?
A: "Man, I'm bushed!"

Q: What is a tornado's favorite game?
A: Twister!

Q: How do mountains greet each other?
A: "High!"

KNOCK, KNOCK!

KNOCK, KNOCK!
  Who's there?
WATER.
  Water who?
WATER YOU DOING IN THERE?

KNOCK, KNOCK!
  Who's there?
WENDY.
  Wendy who?
WENDY TODAY, CLOUDY TOMORROW!

KNOCK, KNOCK!
  Who's there?
TREE.
  Tree who?
HAVE A TREE-RIFFIC DAY!

PUNNY STUFF

Q: What kind of flowers grow on your face?
A: Tulips!

Q: Why are volcanoes so popular?
A: Because they're so lava-ble!

Q: Where does seaweed look for a job?
A: In the kelp wanted section!

Q: Why was the rock braver than the pebble?
A: Because it was a little boulder!

Q: What do trees do when they meet the king?
A: They bough!

GREEN ENERGY

During an interview, the famous scientist was asked to name his favorite type of alternative energy.

"Well, actually, I'm obsessed with wind farms," he admitted.

"Really?"

"Yes. I'm a huge fan!"

MONSTROUSLY FUNNY

The monster-related jokes in this section are so funny, it's scary! They'll tickle your funny bone for sure.

Q: What did the skeleton order for dinner?
A: Spare ribs!

Q: What do vegan zombies eat?
A: Graaaaaaains!

Q: Where do ghosts like to go swimming?
A: Lake Eerie!

Q: Why won't skeletons skydive?
A: They don't have the guts!

Q: What streets do ghosts like to haunt?
A: Dead ends!

Q: Why won't anyone kiss Dracula?
A: He has bat breath!

Q: Which monster loves to dance?
A: The boogie man!

Q: What kind of horses do ghosts ride?
A: Night mares!

Q: Where do monsters go when they're sick?
A: To the witch doctor!

Q: Why did the vampires meet at the cave?
A: They wanted to hang out!

Q: Did you hear that Dracula has a new girlfriend?
A: It was love at first bite!

Q: Why is it safe to tell a mummy your secrets?
A: They're good at keeping things under wraps!

Q: Why did the zombie skip school?
A: He felt rotten!

Q: What do monsters read in the newspaper?
A: The horror-scope!

KNOCK, KNOCK!

KNOCK, KNOCK!
  Who's there?
BOO.
  Boo who?
DON'T CRY—I'M NOT A GHOST!

KNOCK, KNOCK!
  Who's there?
IVANA.
  Ivana who?
IVANA SUCK YOUR BLOOD!

KNOCK, KNOCK!
  Who's there?
WANDA.
  Wanda who?
WANDA RIDE ON MY BROOMSTICK?

PUNNY STUFF

Q: What do monsters turn on in the summertime?
A: Scare conditioners!

Q: Which monster eats the fastest?
A: The goblin!

Q: What did the art critics say about Frankenstein's painting?
A: It was a monsterpiece!

Q: What do ghosts eat for dessert?
A: I scream!

Q: What was the little monster's favorite ride?
A: The scary-go-round!

ON THE MENU

A monster walks into a restaurant.

"How much do you charge for dinner?" it asks the waiter.

"It's $20 a head, sir," the waiter replies.

"And how much more if I wanted a few fingers and legs as well?"

KA-CHING!

Do you want to add to your jackpot of jokes?
No problem—just make them up!
A good joke uses words in unexpected ways to deliver a funny answer. This page lists several possible topics, along with words related to each topic. Use these words as inspiration to invent your own jokes, or come up with your own topics and words. It's absolutely free—but the results will be comedy gold!

Computers: byte, screen, type, key, click, disc, drive, port, mouse, plug
Holidays: tree, egg, gift, day, present, wait, time, play, guess, decorate
Music: song, sing, play, strum, bang, toot, blow, blast, loud, bass
Movies: film, actor, act, role, script, scene, credit, write, shoot, part
Jungles: green, leaf, lush, thick, heat, humid, rain, wild, bush, vine